W9-BCX-918

921
Joh

McKissack, Patricia.

James Weldon Johnson

DATE DUE

JAMES WELDON JOHNSON
"Lift Every Voice and Sing"

JAMES WELDON JOHNSON
"Lift Every Voice and Sing"

By Patricia and Fredrick McKissack
Consulting Editor: Sondra K. Wilson, Ph.D.
President of the Johnson Memorial Foundation

CHILDRENS PRESS®
CHICAGO

James Weldon Johnson is at the bottom right in this school picture.

Library of Congress Cataloging-in-Publication Data

McKissack, Patricia, 1944-
   James Weldon Johnson : "Lift every voice and sing" / by
Patricia and Fredrick McKissack.
      p.   cm. — (A Picture story biography)
   Summary: Recounts the life of the author and civil rights
leader who blazed a trail for racial equality and human rights
through his songs, poems, speeches, and other writings.
   ISBN 0-516-04174-6
   1.   Johnson, James Weldon, 1871-1938—Biography—
Juvenile literature.   2.   Civil rights workers—United
States—Biography—Juvenile literature.   [1.   Johnson,
James Weldon, 1871-1938.   2.   Authors, American.
3.   Civil rights workers.   4.   Afro-Americans—
Biography.]   I.   McKissack, Fredrick.
II.   Title.   III.   Series.
PS3519.02625Z78   1990
818'.5209   89-77273
[92]   CIP
                                                      AC

PHOTO CREDITS

Bettmann Archive—6, 7, (2 photos), 9, 11 (right), 27 (left),
   28 (right)

Fisk University—1, 2, 22, 29, 30

Historical Picture Service, Chicago—5, 11 (left), 12 (both
   photos), 20, 27 (top), 27 (right), 28 (left)

Yale University, Beinecke Library—4, 15 (all photos), 16, 17,
   18 (both photos), 23, 24, 25 (both photos), 26

Courtesy of the James Weldon Johnson Memorial
   Foundation, Inc., Sondra Kathryn Wilson, president—32

Cover and interior by Sara Shelton.

Children play outside their homes in Jacksonville, Florida, in 1896.

A group of young men in Jacksonville, Florida, were planning a celebration for Abraham Lincoln's birthday. They asked James Weldon Johnson, the principal of the black school, to speak.

James wanted to do more than just give a dull speech. He asked his talented brother, Rosamond, for help. The Johnson brothers decided to write a song. James would write the words and Rosamond would compose the music.

James began his work first. He wrote what he believed and felt in his heart.

The slavery years had been cruel. Yet his people had never lost their

faith. They lifted their voices in song and prayer.

Now the years of slavery were ended. There was much to be joyful about. Now black people were supposed to be free and equal to all other Americans. Color was not supposed to matter anymore.

These African-American cavalry soldiers (below), photographed in 1895, were called Buffalo soldiers. Abraham Lincoln freed the slaves.

Lift ev'ry voice and sing
Till earth and heaven ring,
Ring with the harmonies of
  Liberty;
Let our rejoicing rise
High as the list'ning skies,
Let it resound loud as the
  rolling sea.
Sing a song full of the faith that
  the dark past has taught us.
Sing a song full of the hope that
  the present has brought us.
Facing the rising sun
Of our new day begun,
Let us march on till victory is won.

The first stanza was finished.
Then Rosamond composed the
music. He played the melody over
and over.

James listened, letting the music lead him. Words began to tumble out of his mouth. Later, he wrote them down.

Blacks had come a long way since slavery. Making progress had not been easy. Groups like the Ku Klux Klan had made it even harder.

A meeting of the Ku Klux Klan, a racist organization

Clearly, James was proud of his
race. It shows in the uplifting words
in the second stanza.

Stony the road we trod,
Bitter the chast'ning rod,
Felt in the days when hope
   unborn had died;
Yet with a steady beat,
Have not our weary feet
Come to the place for which our
   fathers sighed?
We have come over a way that
   with tears has been watered;
We have come, treading our path
   thro' the blood of the slaughtered,
Out from the gloomy past,
Till now we stand at last
Where the white gleam of our
   bright star is cast.

Jim Crow laws required the separation of blacks and whites. Black and white prisoners even had separate visiting hours.

By 1900, ideas had changed. Color *did* matter. Southern states were passing unjust laws and African-Americans were losing their rights. Would the federal laws protect them? Sadly, the answer was no. Even the United States Supreme Court didn't help.

Black people and white people were separated in buses and theaters under Jim Crow laws.

Soon blacks couldn't go to school with whites. Blacks and whites couldn't work or play together. They couldn't live side by side, or ride in the same train car. In Birmingham, Alabama, it was even against the law for blacks and whites to play checkers together.

James didn't want his people to lose hope. His third stanza is filled with encouraging words.

God of our weary years,
God of our silent tears,
Thou who hast brought us thus
  far on the way;
Thou who hast by Thy might,
Led us into the light,
Keep us forever in the path,
  we pray.
Lest our feet stray from the
  places, our God, where we
  met Thee
Lest our hearts, drunk with the
  wine of the world, we
  forget Thee;
Shadowed beneath Thy Hand,
May we forever stand
True to our God, True to our
  native land.

The song was finished. James was excited and deeply moved. ''I could not keep back the tears,'' he said, ''and made no effort to do so.''

Five hundred Jacksonville schoolchildren sang ''Lift Every Voice and Sing'' for the first time in 1900.

Twenty years later, it was being sung all over the country. The National Association for the Advancement of Colored People (NAACP) made it their theme song. It was called the Negro National Anthem.

''Nothing,'' Johnson wrote later, ''that I have done has paid me back so fully in satisfaction as being part creator of this song.''

James Weldon Johnson loved writing. But he did much more. He was an educator, a lawyer, a diplomat, and a civil rights leader, too. His experiences helped him become a great writer.

In 1933, he wrote his autobiography, *Along This Way.* In this book, he tells about his interesting life.

James Weldon was born on June 17, 1871, in Jacksonville. His brother, John Rosamond, was born two years later. His father, James,

Helen Louise Johnson

James Weldon Johnson
2 years old

James Johnson

was a headwaiter in one of the South's finest hotels. His mother, Helen Louise, was the first female African-American teacher in the state of Florida. The Johnsons were loving, caring parents.

Mrs. Johnson read to her sons. She taught them music and Spanish.

Mr. Johnson worked long hours. The boys were usually asleep when he came home. When they woke in the morning, he was gone. But often they found raisins and fruit under

James Weldon Johnson attended and also taught at the Stanton School.

James Weldon Johnson (top right) was principal of Stanton
High School.

their pillows. It was Mr. Johnson's
special way of showing love.

James Weldon was graduated with
honors from Atlanta University in
1894. Then he served as the
principal of Stanton School in
Jacksonville. It was a challenge. But
his hard work and high standards
paid off. Because of James Weldon's
efforts, Stanton became
Jacksonville's first black high
school.

James Weldon Johnson at age 15 (left). The Atlanta University Quartet (below). Johnson is on the right.

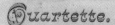

Atlanta University Quartette.

James liked challenges. At that time, there were no black lawyers in Florida. A white friend, Attorney Thomas A. Ledwith, helped James study law. James studied and studied. But could he pass the bar exam? A lot of people didn't think a black could be a lawyer.

A committee of three white lawyers and a white judge tested James. The questions were very difficult. Sometimes they were even unfair. Being well-prepared helped. James answered every question correctly.

One committee member was so resentful that he walked out of the room. It didn't matter. James Weldon Johnson had become the first black in Florida's history to pass the bar exam!

James and Rosamond spent
summers in New York. They met
the famous poet, Paul Laurence
Dunbar. He and James became good
friends. James later wrote:

"I was drawn to him and he to
me; and a friendship was begun that
grew closer and lasted until his
death."

Paul Laurence Dunbar

Dunbar wrote beautiful poetry in standard English and in black dialect. James was inspired to write "Sence You Went Away," his first dialect poem.

Seems lak to me de stars don't
   shine so bright,
Seems lak to me de sun done
   loss his light,
Seems lak to me der's nothin'
   goin' right,
Sence you went away.

Jacksonville was a small town. Opportunities were few. It was time for James and Rosamond to move on.

In 1901, the Johnson brothers moved to New York. They formed a musical group with Bob Cole. There they became successful songwriters.

Known as Cole and the Johnson
Brothers, they traveled to the West
Coast and to Europe.

Below: James Weldon Johnson with his friend Bob Cole (left)
and his brother Rosamond (right). Opposite page: A 1904
photograph of Bob Cole (left), James Weldon Johnson (right),
and Rosamond Johnson (center).

Congo Love Song
Along the Con-go — flows to the sea
Mandy
The Maiden With The Dreamy
W. Anderson
New York
Jan 1 1904
The Maid of Timbuctoo
The maid of Timbuc-too — She knew just what to do
The Owl & the Moon
No body lookin' — but de owl an de moon
Bob Cole
Jas. W. Johnson

Everything was going well in New York. But, before long, James grew restless again. He wrote for a newspaper and studied drama and literature at Columbia University. And between 1906 and 1913, he was appointed U.S. consul to Venezuela and later to Nicaragua.

James Weldon Johnson inspects the troops in Nicaragua.

American Consulate in Corinto, Nicaragua

Grace Nail Johnson

His life was exciting and full of
adventure. But he was lonely. Then
he married Grace Nail. And he said
his life was filled with joy.

James joined the NAACP in 1916.
He was the organization's first black

James Weldon Johnson was named executive secretary of the NAACP.

leader. He was named executive secretary.

Meanwhile, the race problem in America was worse than ever. There were many race riots and lynchings in 1919. So much blood was shed that James Weldon Johnson called it the Red Summer.

Police tend a black victim of the 1919 race riots in Chicago (above).
Blacks marched in New York in 1917 to protest lynchings (below left).

IS THIS CIVILIZATION

Congress,
Give us the right
to vote under the 14th
and 15th Amendments

The Chicago Daily Tribune. FINAL EDITION

FULL CONFESSION BY SLAYER OF JANET

Report Two Killed, Fifty Hurt, in Race Riots

FITZGERALD POINTS OUT GIRL'S BODY UNDER COAL

The Chicago Daily Tribune. FINAL EDITION

STRIKE IS ON; CARS STOP!

20 SLAIN IN RACE RIOTS

The Chicago Daily Tribune. FINAL EDITION

RIOTS SPREAD, THEN WANE

UNION CAR CHIEFS PLAN REFERENDUM

ONE DEATH IN 14 HOURS PUTS TOTAL AT 26

The Chicago Daily Tribune. FINAL EDITION

TROOPS ACT: HALT RIOTING

African-Americans held an equal-rights demonstration in New York City in 1912 to protest lynching and other injustices.

James wanted to stop the senseless lynchings of black men and women. He pushed for Congress to pass the Dyer Antilynching Bill. The bill passed in the House of Representatives, but failed in the Senate in December of 1922.

He won many honors and awards for his fight against lynching. There was still more work to be done. But

Johnson (left) at a Fisk University graduation ceremony

he retired from the NAACP in 1930.

Johnson always found time to write. Writing made him happy. His first novel was *The Autobiography of an Ex-Colored Man.* In 1922 he collected poems written by other black poets in *The Book of American Negro Poetry.* With his brother Rosamond, he published two collections of Negro spirituals. *God's Trombones*, published in 1927, is a

Johnson and fellow teachers at Fisk University

collection of sermons in verse, written in the voice of a black preacher on a Southern plantation.

James's last years were spent as a professor at Fisk University in Nashville, Tennessee. He also was the first black professor at New

York University. He died on June 26, 1938, in an automobile accident in Maine.

James Weldon Johnson is best remembered as the author of "Lift Every Voice and Sing." He wouldn't mind. He said, "I am always thrilled deeply when I hear it sung. . ."

Out from the gloomy past.
Till now we stand at last
Where the white gleam of our
bright star is cast.

When people sing these stirring words, something wonderful happens. Our spirits are uplifted. And our hearts are filled with hope, courage, love, and joy. There is no greater way to be remembered.

Mr. and Mrs. James Weldon Johnson
in 1934

JAMES WELDON JOHNSON

TIMELINE

1871	Born in Jacksonville, Florida, June 17
1894	Graduated from Atlanta University
1897	First black admitted to Florida bar
1899	Wrote "Lift Every Voice and Sing" with brother Rosamond
1906	U.S. consul, Puerto Cabello, Venezuela
1909	U.S. consul, Corinto, Nicaragua
1920	Appointed executive secretary of NAACP
1930	Became professor at Fisk University
1933	Wrote autobiography, *Along This Way*
1938	Died in automobile accident in Maine

INDEX

About the Consulting Editor

Dr. Sondra Kathryn Wilson, president of The Johnson Memorial Foundation in New York City, has written several articles on James Weldon Johnson. Dr. Wilson is also the editor of the James Weldon Johnson Papers.

About the Authors

Patricia C. McKissack and her husband, Fredrick, are free-lance writers, editors, and teachers of writing. They are the owners and operators of All-Writing Services, located in Clayton, Missouri. Ms. McKissack, an award-winning author and experienced educator, has taught writing at several St. Louis colleges and universities.